I·N·S·I·D·E DK G·U·I·D·E·S

INCREDIBLE EARTH

Written by
NICK CLIFFORD

DORLING KINDERSLEY
London • New York • Stuttgart • Moscow

A DORLING KINDERSLEY BOOK

Project Editor Roderick Craig
Art Editor Mark Haygarth
Senior art editor Diane Klein
Managing editor Gillian Denton
Managing art editor Julia Harris
Picture Research Jo Carlill
Production Charlotte Traill

Photography Andy Crawford, Ranald Mackechnie
Modelmakers Chris Reynolds and the
team at BBC Visual Effects

First published in Great Britain in 1996
by Dorling Kindersley Limited,
9 Henrietta Street, London WC2E 8PS

A CIP catalogue record for this book is
available from the British Library.
ISBN 0751 3 54376

Reproduced in Italy by G.R.B. Graphica, Verona
Printed in Singapore by Toppan

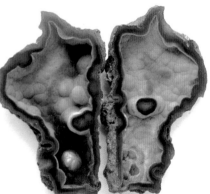

Coral sea fan

Model showing the
Earth's anatomy

Opal sealed in
a nodule of iron

Saharan fringe-toed lizard

Iceshelf
and icebergs

Emperor penguin,
Antarctic resident

Slice through
a stalagmite

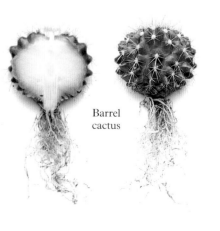

Agate-lined rock cavity

Barrel
cactus

Contents

Tropical fish

Green sea slug

Model of waterfall and river rapids

Crust to core

Imagine a journey to the centre of the Earth, starting at the crust, which is extremely thin, especially under the oceans. From its rocky strata we derive minerals, ores, and fossil fuels. Even heat trapped underground can be harnessed and used in industry and to warm our homes. Going on down, you would see how the movements in the shallower layers beneath the crust are the driving force behind earthquakes and volcanoes, and how they played a part in the creation of the Earth's vast mountain ranges. We still know little about the Earth's deeper layers, but since the 1960s new techniques have improved our understanding of them and of the secrets of how our planet has evolved over millions of years.

All aboard
The Earth's crust is split into eight sections, or plates, which float on a deeper layer known as the mantle.

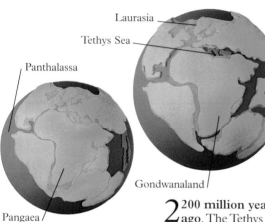

Laurasia
Tethys Sea
India
Panthalassa
South America
Gondwanaland
Pangaea
South Atlantic
Africa

1 **220 million years ago.** A single super-continent floats alone in a vast ocean.

2 **200 million years ago.** The Tethys Sea slowly splits Pangaea into the Gondwanaland and Laurasia masses.

3 **135 million years ago.** Africa and South America appear as Gondwanaland splits.

On the move
The theory of continental drift states that the arrangement of the continents reflects the past movement of the plates on which they lie. So, as the Earth has evolved, the continents, originally joined together, have drifted apart.

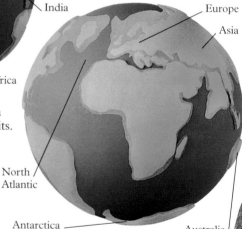

India
Europe
Asia
North Atlantic
Antarctica
Australia

4 **10 million years ago.** The North Atlantic separates Europe and North America. Australia and Antarctica float apart.

Snowy spine
The Himalayas mountain range that dominates Nepal, seen here from space as a long ridge of white peaks, formed as a result of the collision and buckling of the Indian and Asian continental plates. To the right is the high Tibetan Plateau, which was uplifted by the same action.

Meeting plates
As plates move apart along spreading ridges in mid-ocean, new plate material is created by rising lava. Oceanic crust is destroyed where the plates collide. Continental crust "rides" on top of it as it is pushed under, or subducted, into the mantle.

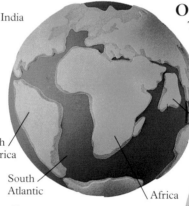

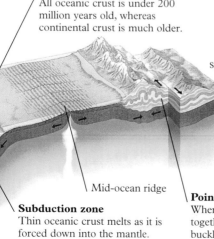

Angry ground
Volcanoes and earthquakes are common in zones of active plate movement.

Old as the sea
All oceanic crust is under 200 million years old, whereas continental crust is much older.

Mid-ocean ridge

Subduction zone
Thin oceanic crust melts as it is forced down into the mantle.

Points of convergence
Where continental plates crash together, long mountain ranges buckle up along fault lines.

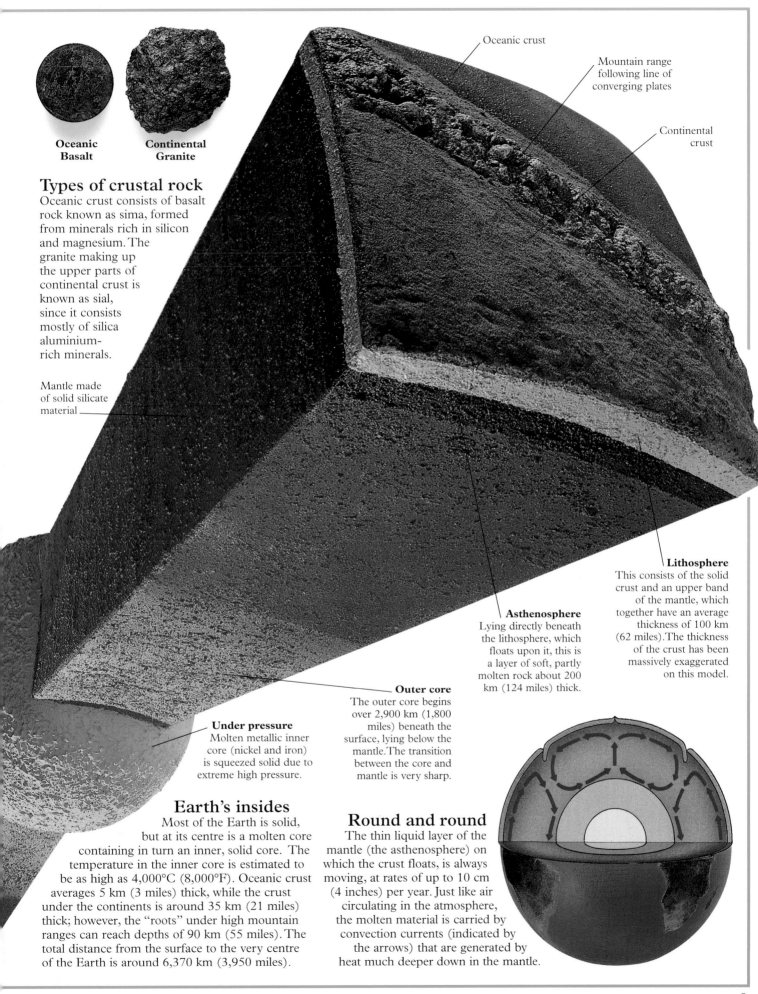

Oceanic Basalt

Continental Granite

Oceanic crust

Mountain range following line of converging plates

Continental crust

Types of crustal rock

Oceanic crust consists of basalt rock known as sima, formed from minerals rich in silicon and magnesium. The granite making up the upper parts of continental crust is known as sial, since it consists mostly of silica aluminium-rich minerals.

Mantle made of solid silicate material

Lithosphere
This consists of the solid crust and an upper band of the mantle, which together have an average thickness of 100 km (62 miles). The thickness of the crust has been massively exaggerated on this model.

Asthenosphere
Lying directly beneath the lithosphere, which floats upon it, this is a layer of soft, partly molten rock about 200 km (124 miles) thick.

Outer core
The outer core begins over 2,900 km (1,800 miles) beneath the surface, lying below the mantle. The transition between the core and mantle is very sharp.

Under pressure
Molten metallic inner core (nickel and iron) is squeezed solid due to extreme high pressure.

Earth's insides

Most of the Earth is solid, but at its centre is a molten core containing in turn an inner, solid core. The temperature in the inner core is estimated to be as high as 4,000°C (8,000°F). Oceanic crust averages 5 km (3 miles) thick, while the crust under the continents is around 35 km (21 miles) thick; however, the "roots" under high mountain ranges can reach depths of 90 km (55 miles). The total distance from the surface to the very centre of the Earth is around 6,370 km (3,950 miles).

Round and round

The thin liquid layer of the mantle (the asthenosphere) on which the crust floats, is always moving, at rates of up to 10 cm (4 inches) per year. Just like air circulating in the atmosphere, the molten material is carried by convection currents (indicated by the arrows) that are generated by heat much deeper down in the mantle.

Wind and water

Looking at the Earth from space, you see a striking blue planet. This is due to the fact that over 70 per cent of its surface is covered by water. This watery layer is known as the hydrosphere, and includes the oceans, lakes, rivers, snow, and icecaps. The water that evaporates into the atmosphere becomes clouds and is important in regulating the Earth's climate, as are the circulating gyres, or currents, within the oceans. Patterns in the winds and weather systems occurring in the atmosphere, of which hurricanes, or typhoons, and tornadoes are the most violent examples, help in turn to maintain the different climatic zones around the world.

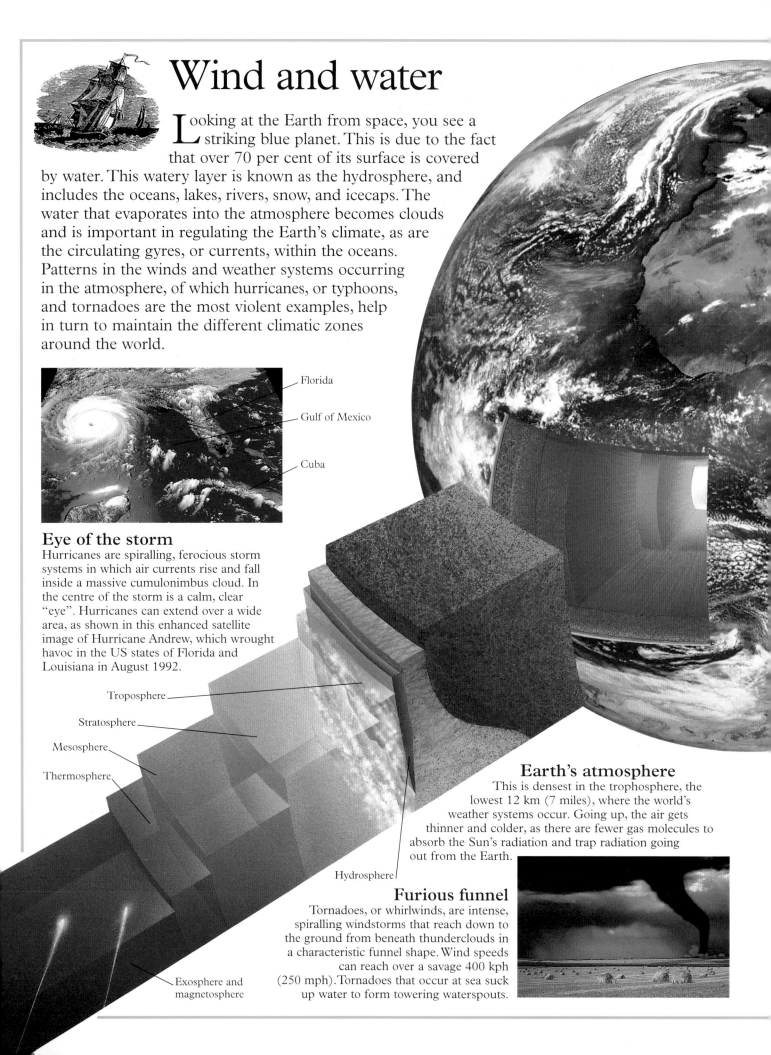

Florida

Gulf of Mexico

Cuba

Eye of the storm

Hurricanes are spiralling, ferocious storm systems in which air currents rise and fall inside a massive cumulonimbus cloud. In the centre of the storm is a calm, clear "eye". Hurricanes can extend over a wide area, as shown in this enhanced satellite image of Hurricane Andrew, which wrought havoc in the US states of Florida and Louisiana in August 1992.

Troposphere

Stratosphere

Mesosphere

Thermosphere

Hydrosphere

Exosphere and magnetosphere

Earth's atmosphere

This is densest in the trophosphere, the lowest 12 km (7 miles), where the world's weather systems occur. Going up, the air gets thinner and colder, as there are fewer gas molecules to absorb the Sun's radiation and trap radiation going out from the Earth.

Furious funnel

Tornadoes, or whirlwinds, are intense, spiralling windstorms that reach down to the ground from beneath thunderclouds in a characteristic funnel shape. Wind speeds can reach over a savage 400 kph (250 mph). Tornadoes that occur at sea suck up water to form towering waterspouts.

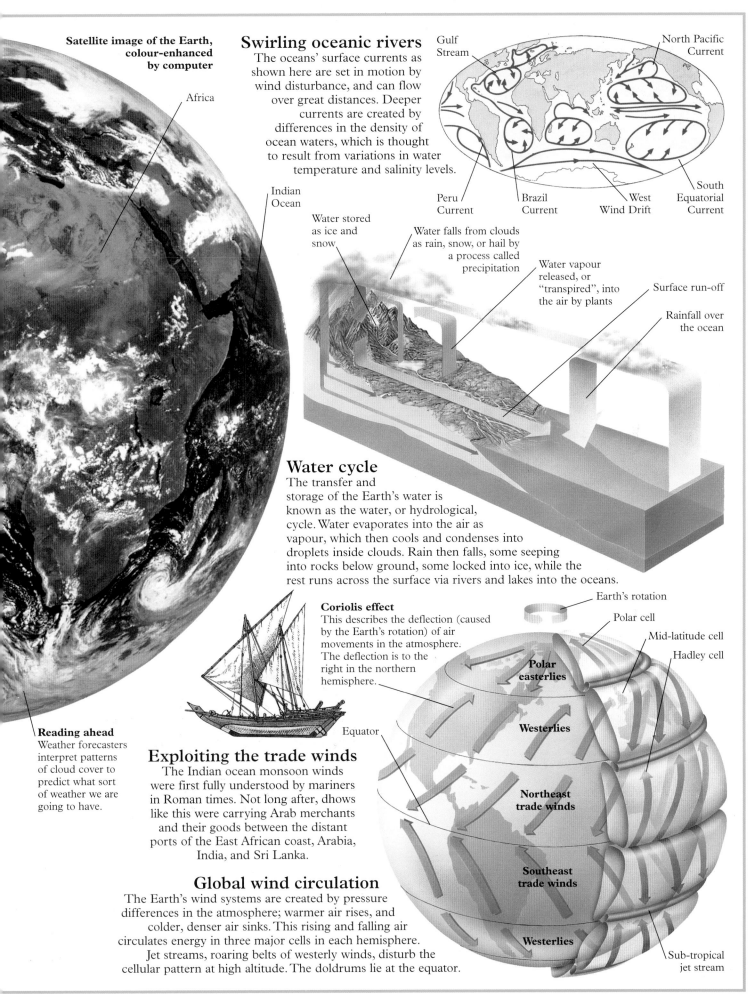

Satellite image of the Earth, colour-enhanced by computer

Africa

Indian Ocean

Swirling oceanic rivers

The oceans' surface currents as shown here are set in motion by wind disturbance, and can flow over great distances. Deeper currents are created by differences in the density of ocean waters, which is thought to result from variations in water temperature and salinity levels.

Gulf Stream

North Pacific Current

Peru Current

Brazil Current

West Wind Drift

South Equatorial Current

Water stored as ice and snow

Water falls from clouds as rain, snow, or hail by a process called precipitation

Water vapour released, or "transpired", into the air by plants

Surface run-off

Rainfall over the ocean

Water cycle

The transfer and storage of the Earth's water is known as the water, or hydrological, cycle. Water evaporates into the air as vapour, which then cools and condenses into droplets inside clouds. Rain then falls, some seeping into rocks below ground, some locked into ice, while the rest runs across the surface via rivers and lakes into the oceans.

Coriolis effect
This describes the deflection (caused by the Earth's rotation) of air movements in the atmosphere. The deflection is to the right in the northern hemisphere.

Equator

Earth's rotation

Polar cell

Mid-latitude cell

Hadley cell

Polar easterlies

Westerlies

Northeast trade winds

Southeast trade winds

Westerlies

Sub-tropical jet stream

Reading ahead
Weather forecasters interpret patterns of cloud cover to predict what sort of weather we are going to have.

Exploiting the trade winds

The Indian ocean monsoon winds were first fully understood by mariners in Roman times. Not long after, dhows like this were carrying Arab merchants and their goods between the distant ports of the East African coast, Arabia, India, and Sri Lanka.

Global wind circulation

The Earth's wind systems are created by pressure differences in the atmosphere; warmer air rises, and colder, denser air sinks. This rising and falling air circulates energy in three major cells in each hemisphere. Jet streams, roaring belts of westerly winds, disturb the cellular pattern at high altitude. The doldrums lie at the equator.

The fossil record

Fossils are the preserved remains or trace evidence of long-dead flora and fauna that have been petrified in rocks or buried under peat, ice, or in ancient tree resins. In most cases, only the skeletal parts of organisms survive, the fleshy tissue having rotted away or been replaced by minerals. Why are fossils significant and what do they tell us about the Earth? Organized into a formal system of classification known as the fossil record, they provide important clues as to the environment and life on Earth way before history began. The study of fossils, called palaeontology, shows that life originated at least 3.5 billion years ago and how it has evolved since then.

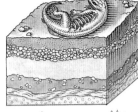

1 An ancient land animal dies and the soft flesh on the carcass starts to decompose where it lies.

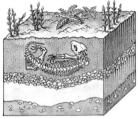

2 The intact skeletal remains are rapidly buried by sediment from shallow streams.

3 The material around the fossil turns into rock over millions of years and is covered with other layers.

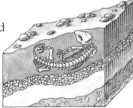

4 As the rock above is eroded away, the fossil is eventually exposed again at the surface.

The fossilization process
This is how organic remains, in this case a small reptile, are typically fossilized. Marine life buried by sediment is exposed later when the seabed is dry, rocky land.

Modern beech leaf

Spiny surface

Diamond pattern

Fossil cone
This very well preserved cone from a monkey puzzle tree was buried by volcanic ash in southern Argentina. Finds like this reveal how the vegetation might have looked.

Seeds inside cut section of cone

Leafy details
Despite the fact that it is around 40 million years old, the veiny texture of this leaf, which is similar to a modern beech leaf, has been preserved in the muddy rock that encased it.

Large, rounded skull vault

Human origins
Using fossil finds like this *Homo habilis* skull, found in Kenya, Africa, experts have been able to piece together the story of the ancestors of fully modern humans.

Homo habilis was typically only 1.2 m (4 ft) tall

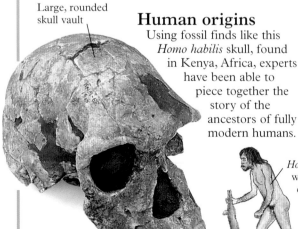

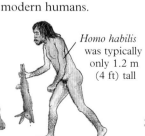

Triceratops
Fossil finds like this skull provide the evidence for the existence of dinosaurs. In some cases, almost complete skeletons have been discovered.

Bony frill on skull for added protection

Toothless beak for tearing plant stems apart

Serrated cutting edges

Tiger shark tooth
Shark teeth are quite common fossils, as are shark scales and dorsal-fin spines. Sharks have skeletons of cartilage, which do not usually survive fossilized.

Oval trilobite

This ancient marine arthropod from Australia is called a trilobite, so named because its body is split into three parts – head shield, thorax, and tail shield. A lobster is a typical example of a modern arthropod.

Typical length 6 cm (2.5 in)

Thorax divided into segments

Tail shield

Large eyes in head shield

Shells with radiating, fine ribs

Bivalve molluscs

Bivalves have two valves, or shell halves, hinged together by a ligament that is rarely preserved in fossils. This is a variety of Glycymeris, or Bitter Sweet, which burrowed into mud or sand in shallow waters.

Ligament attachment area

Typical length 8 cm (3.2 in)

Fanning out
Shell ornamented with broad ribs and radiating growth lines.

Convex right valve

Shell spire
Campanile shells can be up to 60 cm (24 in) long. Main part of body was coiled up and carried inside the shell. The shell is made up of regular whorls.

Ear

Shell made of a form of calcium carbonate called aragonite

Straight hinge line

Central pillar, or columella

Pecten shell

Another bivalve specimen is this scallop shell, with a convex right valve and a flattened left valve. Pecten rested in hollows made in clean sand in relatively shallow water. It swam by rapidly opening and closing the hinged valves. Some Pecten fossils are comparatively recent.

Flattened left valve

Ancient colonies

Colonial animals called bryozoans grew in clumps and bushes on the sea floor. Many grew hard external skeletons like modern corals. This variety of sea mat, called Ceriocava, had long cylindrical branches.

Opening for head with stalked eyes and flattened foot for crawling

Gastropod molluscs

Gastropods were, and still are, very successful, living on land as well as in marine and freshwater habitats. This is the shell of the large gastropod, Campanile, or Giant Serith.

Branches filtered food from water

Cross-section of shell

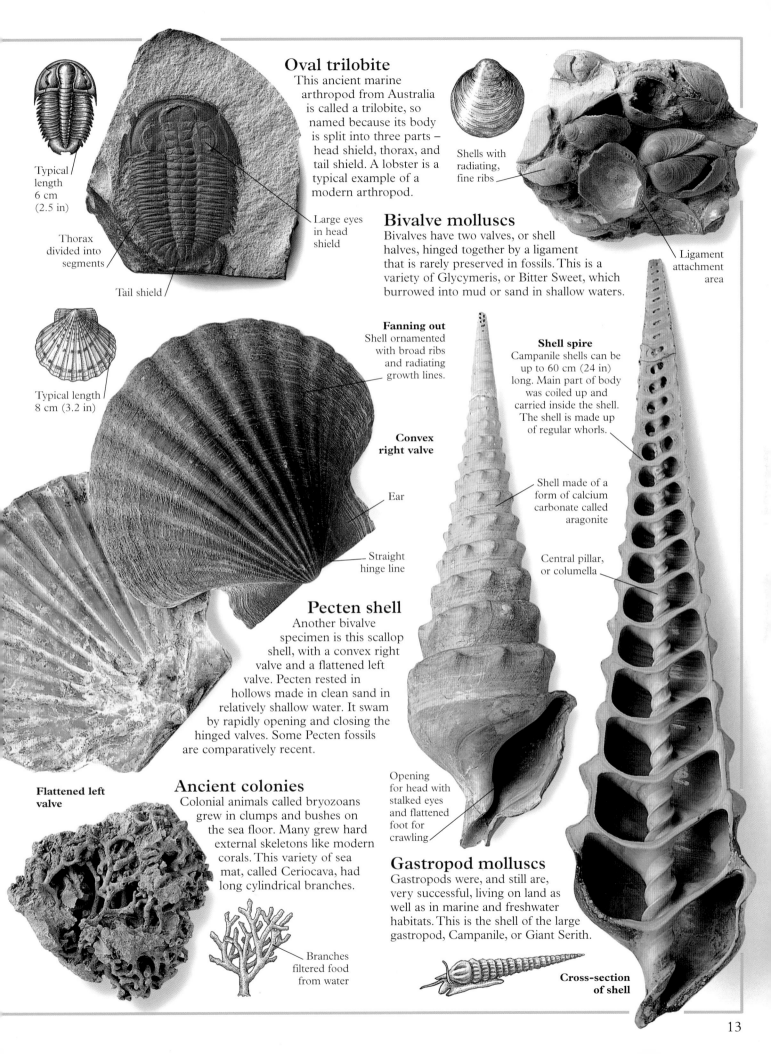

Violent earthquakes

The most destructive, terrifying earthquakes are generated by sudden movements deep in the Earth's crust. They occur where enormous stresses build up in the rocks along fault lines, which are associated with movements of the crustal plates. When the rocks finally snap apart under pressure, the resulting shock waves tear through the land as they travel, often wreaking havoc great distances away. Unfortunately, predicting where and when an earthquake is going to strike is an imprecise science, so those living in danger zones have always to be prepared, and buildings designed to withstand the shocks.

Earth crack
The source of the worst earthquakes in the US state of California has been the San Andreas fault system, seen here spanning the Carrizo Plain in the centre of the state. The distinct kinks in the paths of the river gulleys clearly show the sliding movements along the fault line.

Types of fault
Shown here are five common fault types. Faults range in size from small cracks and escarpments to entire mountain ranges and plateaus.

Urban chaos
The power of an earthquake is measured on the Richter scale. Those measuring 8 and above are especially destructive. The damage in urban areas is often made worse by fires, fallen power cables, and ruptured mains pipes.

Reverse fault

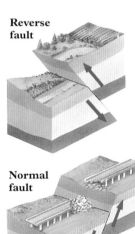

Normal fault

Mind your head
Many deaths and injuries can be caused by masonry and rubble falling from buildings as they collapse.

Horst

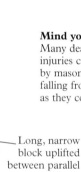

Long, narrow block uplifted between parallel normal faults

Rift valley

Long, narrow sunken block between parallel normal faults

Transform fault

Gaping holes appear where loose earth liquefies

Telephone lines snap and fall

Caught off guard
The US city of Charleston, South Carolina, was hit by a quake in 1886. This is unusual, as the city lies in an almost quake-free zone. But when they do occur, they can be powerful!

Weak construction
These timber houses in San Francisco were built on reclaimed land in the Marina District. During the 1989 earthquake, some literally slipped off their foundations.

Fires and explosions occur where gas pipes burst and electricity cables hit the ground

Earthquakes can be very dangerous if there is a lot of traffic on the roads

Freeway concertina
One of the many tragic scenes in the aftermath of the 1989 San Francisco Loma Prieta quake was the surprising collapse of this elevated section of the Nimitz Freeway, in which a number of motorists were killed.

Built to last
Buildings with stronger foundations or more flexible structure tend to remain intact, although windows are likely to shatter

Folds form in the ground as the earth heaves to and fro

Fault line along which both sides have moved in opposite directions

Gathering momentum
Tsunami travels at great speed in a low, broad sweep across the deep ocean surface. Its height increases dramatically as it enters a shallower coastal zone.

Walls of water
Earthquakes that occur far beneath the oceans can cause towering tidal waves, or tsunamis. These can reach over 60 m (197 ft) high when they hit shallow water and cause catastrophic flooding as they batter the shoreline.

Focal point of quake, or epicentre, located along fault in ocean floor

Volcanoes

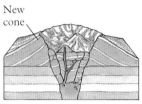

This engraving shows the eruption of Mount Pelée in Martinique, on 5 August, 1851.

Perhaps the most awe-inspiring and menacing features of the Earth's surface, volcanoes have long represented the mighty power of nature and the gods. Forming above pipe-like vents or fissures through which molten rock, or magma, is forced to the surface, there are, today, around 600 volcanoes on land. Some are active, some dormant, while many more exist in the depths of the oceans. Eruptions can be either violent, ejecting huge amounts of lava, ash, and gas high into the sky, or much gentler, oozing long flows of runny lava.

Road to nowhere
Massive lava flows destroy everything in their path, like the village that once lay at the end of this road near Mount Kilauea volcano in Hawaii.

Types of volcano
Pictured to the left are the six kinds of volcano. Violent eruptions are common to the ash-cinder, caldera, and composite types, while the others produce runny lava that quickly spreads and cools over a wide area. Some volcanoes combine features of each variety.

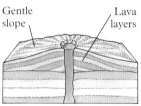

New cone

Caldera (crater) volcano

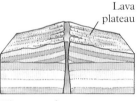

Gentle slope

Lava layers

Basic shield volcano

Lava plateau

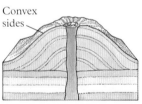

Fissure volcano

Convex sides

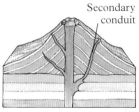

Dome volcano

Secondary conduit

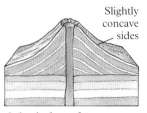

Composite volcano

Slightly concave sides

Ash-cinder volcano

Flattened out
Repeated lava flows bury surrounding land and can form an extensive volcanic plateau over millions of years.

Rough surface
The barren sides and base of the cone are littered with brittle lumps of cooled lava, ash, and pumice stone.

Layer upon layer
Rings of ash and rock from successive eruptions build up the steep sides of the volcano cone over time.

Bite-sized lava fragments

Blown to pieces
The ferocity of escaping magma gases pulverizes the rock at the top of a volcanic vent. The ejected material is know as tephra and varies in size from gravelly chunks to vast "bombs" as big as houses.

Smaller ash cinders

Ash dust

Fiery furnace
This model represents an active composite volcano, with a large central vent and some secondary conduits. Its steep-sided cone is built up in layers of ash and acidic lava that correspond to different phases of eruption.

Heart of Fire
Central vent spews
out ash, sulphurous
gases, and fireballs
of molten rock.

Pillar of ash
The eruption of Mount
St Helen's, in Washington
State, USA, in May 1980,
ejected a column of fine
dust 20 km (13 miles)
high. Gas and ash raced
down its sides at huge
speed, devastating land
25 km (16 miles) away.

Side eruption
Lava pours out of a
secondary conduit, or dyke,
topped by a small cone.

Patch of yellow
sulphur crystals

Lava "sill"
Channel of lava that squeezed its way up
between the older layers, forming a band
of black, glassy obsidian rock as it cooled.

Trees catch
fire as lava
approaches

"Pahoehoe" flow
Surface of lava flow
covered with ropey
ripples called by their
Hawaiian name.

Bulldozing ahead
New dyke of lava gradually
forces its way up, under
enormous pressure,
towards the surface.

Wings of flame
Curtains of molten
rock branch out from
magma chamber.

Raging torrent
The eruption of Ruiz
Volcano in Colombia, in
November 1985, caused
a slide of melted snow
and ash to charge down
a canyon and destroy the
distant city of Armero,
killing 22,000 people.

Main
magma
chamber

Geyser fields

Otherwise known as hydrothermal areas, geyser fields are home to spectacular phenomena including boiling hot springs, vents spitting out jets of sulphurous gas, cascading sinter terraces, and bubbling mud pools. Geysers, however, are the stars of the show, erupting water and steam in regular cycles. Geyser fields occur at sites of past volcanic activity where moisture is trapped and heated by the energy in subterranean volcanic rocks. These rocks are rich in minerals, which are carried to the surface dissolved in the super-hot water. Such places have long been exploited for the refreshing and healing properties of their mineral-laden springs.

"Old Faithful"
So called because it never fails to erupt on time, this fantastic geyser in Yellowstone National Park, United States, spurts a hot-water fountain 50 m (164 ft) into the air, every 70 minutes or so.

The mineral aphthitalite

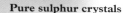

Crusty layers
As hot spring water cools, mineral crusts form at the edges of pools and overflow channels. Likewise, crystal formations, notably sulphur, occur near steam vents.

Large, translucent crystals

Pure sulphur crystals

Simmering mud pot
Where hot spring water mixes with rock particles broken down by acidic gases, bubbling basins of creamy mud are born, like this one in Iceland. The close-up (left) is of a mud pool in the Solfatara crater near Naples, Italy.

"Morning Glory"
Another star of Yellowstone National Park is this pool, famous for the stunning colours of the tiny plants (algae) and bacteria living in its nutrient-rich waters.

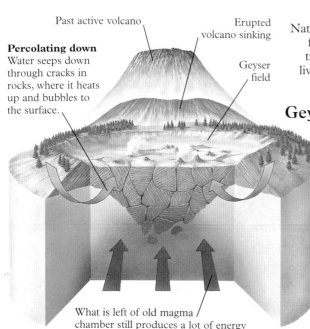

Past active volcano

Percolating down
Water seeps down through cracks in rocks, where it heats up and bubbles to the surface.

Erupted volcano sinking

Geyser field

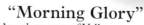

Geyser field formation
Hydrothermal areas, which can reach up to 40 km (25 miles) across, occur in crater depressions where a volcano has gradually collapsed in on itself after erupting violently.

Yellow peril
Spiky sulphur crystals form around the vent entrance.

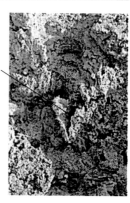

What is left of old magma chamber still produces a lot of energy

Villainous odours
Vents, or fumaroles, like this one at Solfatara, expel invisible plumes of pungent gases which then condense and vaporize. Vents can be noisy, sounding like high-pressure steam engines.

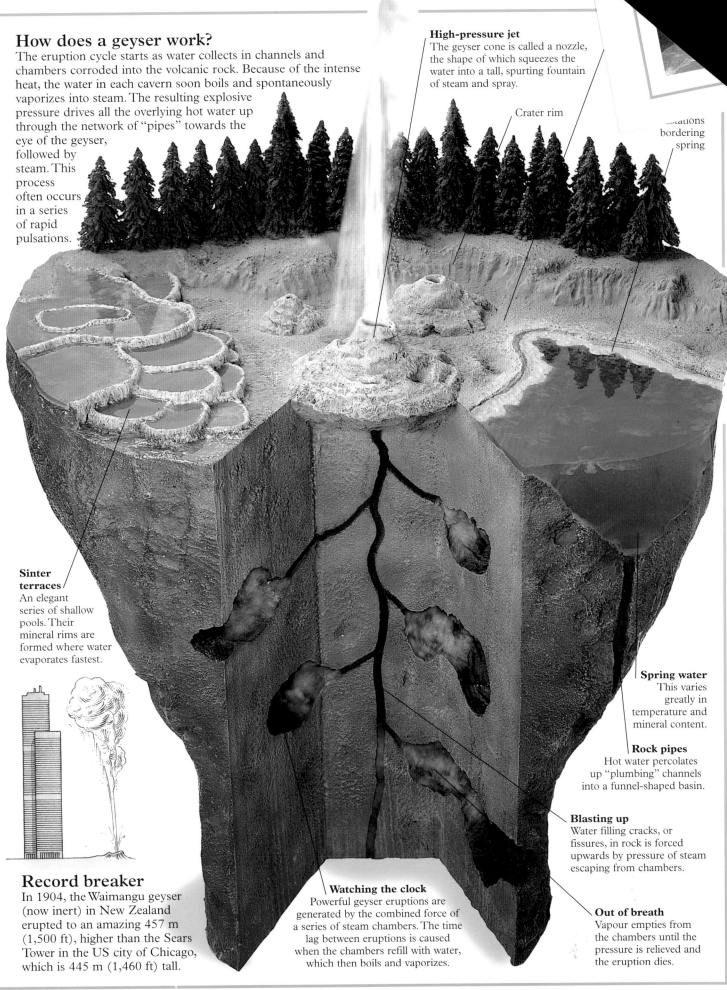

How does a geyser work?

The eruption cycle starts as water collects in channels and chambers corroded into the volcanic rock. Because of the intense heat, the water in each cavern soon boils and spontaneously vaporizes into steam. The resulting explosive pressure drives all the overlying hot water up through the network of "pipes" towards the eye of the geyser, followed by steam. This process often occurs in a series of rapid pulsations.

High-pressure jet
The geyser cone is called a nozzle, the shape of which squeezes the water into a tall, spurting fountain of steam and spray.

Crater rim

...tations bordering spring

Sinter terraces
An elegant series of shallow pools. Their mineral rims are formed where water evaporates fastest.

Spring water
This varies greatly in temperature and mineral content.

Rock pipes
Hot water percolates up "plumbing" channels into a funnel-shaped basin.

Blasting up
Water filling cracks, or fissures, in rock is forced upwards by pressure of steam escaping from chambers.

Record breaker
In 1904, the Waimangu geyser (now inert) in New Zealand erupted to an amazing 457 m (1,500 ft), higher than the Sears Tower in the US city of Chicago, which is 445 m (1,460 ft) tall.

Watching the clock
Powerful geyser eruptions are generated by the combined force of a series of steam chambers. The time lag between eruptions is caused when the chambers refill with water, which then boils and vaporizes.

Out of breath
Vapour empties from the chambers until the pressure is relieved and the eruption dies.

19

Rivers of ice

As well as protruding like icy tongues from the polar icecaps, glaciers also occur at high altitudes in milder regions. These are called valley, or alpine, glaciers. Originating in rounded "cirques", glaciers often combine to form a massive, sluggish flow. For glaciers to survive and grow, more snow must accumulate on the upper reaches than is lost by melting near the ends. This ongoing cycle drives glaciers forwards. Meltwater pipes and chambers beneath a glacier also help it slide over its bed, often in "surges". In Alaska, amazingly, glaciers have been seen to travel several kilometres in only a few days.

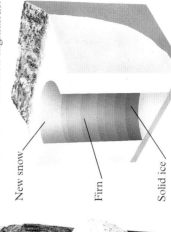

Upstream view
The patterns of crevasses, seen here in the higher, spiky surface of the Arpette glacier in the Swiss Alps, give us important clues as to the internal movements of ice within a glacier.

Sharp spine
This glacially carved jagged ridge is known as an arête.

Snow blanket
Freshly fallen snow covers the upper parts of the glacier.

Medial moraine

After the ice has gone
Glaciers deepen and straighten their host valleys into characteristic U-shaped troughs, like this one viewed from the summit of Cairn Gorm in the Scottish highlands.

New snow

Firn

Solid ice

Snow to ice
As new snow piles up on top of a glacier, the snow beneath it is slowly compacted. With repeated melting and refreezing, "firn" results. The ice at the base has had most of the air squeezed out of it.

Ice fall
Where there are steep drops in the underlying bedrock, the glacier ice breaks up into a series of huge, transverse, step-like crevasses.

Lateral moraine

Head of glacier in cirque

Steep walls
This typical Norwegian fjord is a deep trough carved by a glacier, which was then flooded by the sea after the ice retreated.

Deep fracture
A "bergshrund" crevasse forms as ice is pulled away from the back wall of the cirque under its own weight.

Hanging valley
Here the present glacier has cut right through an earlier valley. In some glacially formed landscapes, dramatic waterfalls result where a river flows over the edge of a hanging valley.

Emerging torrent

Meltwater carries huge amounts of finely ground rock material, as this stream at the snout of the Zinal glacier in Switzerland shows well.

Merging together
Outline of smaller glacier marked by rocks trapped in the ice.

Scraped clean
Bedrock surface scoured and smoothed by boulders embedded in the slow-moving ice.

Streams converge in meltwater pond

Left behind
Ground moraine material deposited by the glacier as it retreats is moulded into various lumpy landscape features.

Moulin

Different speeds
Curved crevasses show how the flow of ice is faster and closer to the surface in the middle of a glacier.

Three steps of a glacier

These models represent the beginning, middle, and end of a typical valley glacier made up of a major and a secondary flow. Rocky debris, known as moraine, carried within the glacial ice, indicates where they join. Lateral moraine accumulates along the valley sides and terminal moraine at the snout, where bouldery gravel lodges along the base.

Meltwater chamber

Ice cave mouth

Gaping chasm
Surface meltwater plunges down a drainage shaft, or moulin, which leads into a network of tubes and chambers at the glacier's base.

Muddy end
Glacier snout is discoloured by fine debris.

Ice continent

Antarctica is the Earth's southernmost and most inhospitable continent, where the average winter temperature is a numbing –60°C (–76°F). Together with the Arctic, its northern twin, the Antarctic ice sheet locks away almost 90 per cent of the world's fresh water into a permanent frozen reservoir. Changes in the size of the ice sheets, which may be many kilometres thick in places, are now monitored by satellites; these show that between summer and winter, ice sheets vary by as much as five times in extent. The coverage and depth of ice is thought to have a distinct effect on the Earth's climate, and intensive studies are now in progress to determine the nature of this relationship.

Permanent ice cover

South Pole

GREATER ANTARCTICA

LESSER ANTARCTICA

Antarctica
Unlike the Arctic, which is a vast oceanic ice sheet, Antarctica is a continent of solid rock ringed by ice. The thick ice at both poles is very old and may preserve a record of past environments.

Tabletops
Some icebergs can be up to 240 km (150 miles) long and 110 km (70 miles) wide. Gargantuan flat-topped, or "tabular", icebergs like this one, break off the iceshelves lining the edges of the continent.

In the freezer
The thickness of the Antarctic icecap has built up over thousands of years, as fresh layers of snow have gradually been compacted. The ice slowly flows, or deforms, out towards the sea under its own weight, forming vast buoyant shelves lined by dramatic, sheer ice cliffs.

HMS *Endurance*, flagship vessel of the British Antarctic Survey

As icebergs are attacked by wave action, deep ice caves can often be created at the waterline

Pack ice

Floating ice raft
During the short summer season, packs of crabeater seals are a common sight along Antarctic shorelines. Here a small group basks lazily in the sunshine on a drifting icefloe.

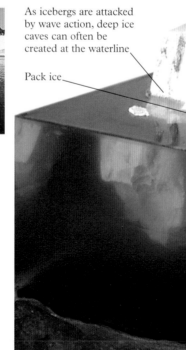

Basic necessity
Krill, shrimp-like crustaceans just 5 cm (2 in) long, are a vital food source for whales, seals, penguins, and seabirds.

Ice sculptures

As icebergs melt and are eroded by the action of wind and waves, weird and wonderful shapes and patterns in the ice can be produced.

Head for heights

Icebergs can reach dizzying heights. One Arctic berg, spotted in 1958, was higher than St Paul's Cathedral in London.

Blue glass

Some icebergs can appear blue as they reflect the water around them. Here the ice has been transformed into what look like huge frosted-glass bottles.

Birth of an iceberg
Vast icy pillar generates huge waves as it "calves" off the main shelf.

Jagged peaks
High mountaintops jutting through the surface of the icecap are called nunataks.

Polar ice may be many kilometres thick

Huge crevasses scour surface of ice sheet as it moves and cracks internally

Ice and rock material scrapes over bedrock as it moves

Emperor penguins

Over two-thirds of an iceberg's bulk are hidden below water

Seabed littered with bouldery gravel and silt deposited by melting icebergs

Thermal gear

Penguins have tough feathers and thick blubber to keep out the Antarctic cold. Their teeming, noisy, summer breeding colonies are a spectacular sight.

Ocean depths

Shrouded in mystery, the ocean floors remain largely unexplored. From the shallow edges, or shelves, of the continents, they descend dramatically, levelling off into ocean basins that may be up to 6 km (3.5 miles) below the surface. Oceanic trenches plunge even deeper – up to a staggering 11 km (7 miles). This strange undersea world conceals huge plains, mountain ranges, volcanoes, and canyons that dwarf anything seen on land. Whatever life exists has adapted to two extremes: the enormous pressure exerted by the weight of water above, and the total absence of light.

"Black smokers"
These strange features perch like chimneys on top of hydrothermal vents, cracks in the ocean floor where seawater gushes up, having been heated by hot volcanic rocks below. First found in 1977, vents occur close to volcanic rifts in the seabed.

Super-hot water cools as it emerges

Poisonous jets
The sulphurous water is highly toxic, but vent-site wildlife has adapted uniquely by surviving on bacteria which flourish on the toxic compounds.

Moulded mounds
Smokers, which can be up to 10m (33 ft) tall, are built up by minerals dissolved in the gushing water. The minerals solidify and accumulate as the water cools.

Red-tipped tentacles
These giant tube worms were photographed at a vent near the Galapagos Islands in the eastern Pacific. Typical vent-site residents, they can be up to 3 m (10 ft) long. For food they depend on bacteria living inside their trunk-like bodies, which they in turn supply with hydrogen sulphide and other chemicals extracted from the gaseous vent water.

Tube-worm tentacle

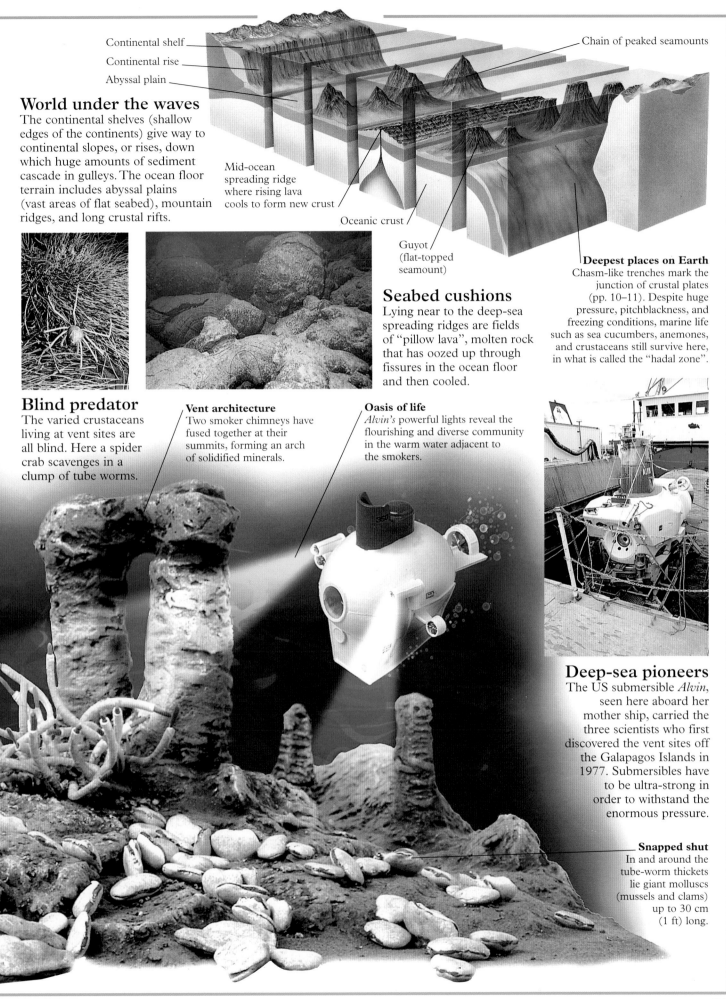

World under the waves

The continental shelves (shallow edges of the continents) give way to continental slopes, or rises, down which huge amounts of sediment cascade in gulleys. The ocean floor terrain includes abyssal plains (vast areas of flat seabed), mountain ridges, and long crustal rifts.

Continental shelf

Continental rise

Abyssal plain

Chain of peaked seamounts

Mid-ocean spreading ridge where rising lava cools to form new crust

Oceanic crust

Guyot (flat-topped seamount)

Seabed cushions

Lying near to the deep-sea spreading ridges are fields of "pillow lava", molten rock that has oozed up through fissures in the ocean floor and then cooled.

Deepest places on Earth

Chasm-like trenches mark the junction of crustal plates (pp. 10–11). Despite huge pressure, pitchblackness, and freezing conditions, marine life such as sea cucumbers, anemones, and crustaceans still survive here, in what is called the "hadal zone".

Blind predator

The varied crustaceans living at vent sites are all blind. Here a spider crab scavenges in a clump of tube worms.

Vent architecture

Two smoker chimneys have fused together at their summits, forming an arch of solidified minerals.

Oasis of life

Alvin's powerful lights reveal the flourishing and diverse community in the warm water adjacent to the smokers.

Deep-sea pioneers

The US submersible *Alvin*, seen here aboard her mother ship, carried the three scientists who first discovered the vent sites off the Galapagos Islands in 1977. Submersibles have to be ultra-strong in order to withstand the enormous pressure.

Snapped shut

In and around the tube-worm thickets lie giant molluscs (mussels and clams) up to 30 cm (1 ft) long.

Towering cliffs

Rocky coasts are a battleground between the attacking waves of the sea and the defending forces of the land. Cliffs, under attack near their bases, remain sheer owing to frequent rockfalls. Over time, their changing outline is determined by the kind of rock that makes them up. Rock that is layered and jointed gives rise to dramatic stack and arch formations, while that formed from muds and gravels is eroded away rapidly. Beaches are the result of eroded material accumulating at the shoreline; steep, narrow, "storm" beaches are common at the foot of sea cliffs and in rounded bays.

Vertical cut-off
These plunging limestone cliffs stretch for miles and miles along the edge of the Nullarbor Plain, a vast, flat plateau in South Australia.

Mariners' friend
Standing robustly at the summit of jutting headlands, lighthouses like this one near Holyhead in Anglesey, North Wales, warn sailors to steer clear of the rocks at the foot of the cliffs.

Debris cone
Rockfalls contribute to slow process of cliff retreat.

Jagged edge
Cliff face is marked with crags and gulleys where boulders fall.

Storm waves eat away at cliff base

Water spurts up through blowhole when sea is rough

Cave mouth

Extended platform

1 Here the sea has already eroded its way deep into the cliffs of this imaginary coastline, sculpting patterns of more and less resistant rock into an impressive arch.

Beaches form in more protected areas

Gulls galore
Noisy seagulls are a typical sight flying over coastal cliffs.

Hard floor
Wave-cut shore platforms, or terraces, form at the base of the cliffs, where the sea's attack is most effective.

Arch roof slowly degrades

Stack

2 As storm waves exert their erosive force, the cliff retreats over time. The roof of the first sea arch has collapsed, leaving a lone pillar, or stack. Another arch has appeared behind it.

Cove to bays
The sea starts by finding weak points in the cliffs, then goes on to carve out coves in the less resistant rock behind. Slowly, wide, curving bays are excavated. More resistant rock forms islands and protruding headlands.

Weak spot in cliff

Waves gradually wear down sides of cove

Deposited rock debris forms beaches

Tombolo in the making
Eroded material transported along the shore may re-join islands to the coast, creating a tombolo.

Deceptively docile
Now the sea is calm and at low tide, belying the fact that any minute the wind can stir up powerful waves, which hurl themselves mercilessly at the cliffs.

Larger stones and pebbles

3 Now the coastline has moved backwards some distance. The only evidence of its original position are two towering stacks. The cave and blowhole show that the present cliff is still being excavated by water action and cavitation by air trapped in the rocks.

First stack continually being worn down

Gritty sand

Rocks to sand
Beyond the bouldery rocks at the foot of cliffs, beach material gradually gets finer as the grains wear each other away.

Boulders carried away from beach by waves

Fine sand

Tombolo

Where cliffs once stood
Where cliffs once stood, wave-cut platforms of resistant rock often remain, as seen in the foreground of this stretch of coast near the Cape of Good Hope in South Africa.

Coral reefs

Colourful and swarming with life, coral reefs are the marine gardens of the tropical oceans. Reefs result from the accumulation of limestone, created by the hard outer skeletons of tiny animals called polyps. Although reefs can be very broad and plunge hundreds of metres deep, only their upper sections are alive, as corals can only survive in warm, shallow water. Also, the microscopic plants, called algae, that grow with corals, are sensitive to the amount of sunlight penetrating the water; below a few metres, they cannot function. Reef conservation is a major ecological aim, as many are under threat from tourism and pollution.

Sleek and deadly
Graceful reef sharks stalk their prey in the plentiful hunting grounds of reef edges.

Pacific paradise

Kayangell Atoll, in the Palau group of the Caroline Islands, is a typical ring-shaped coral atoll with verdant coral islands shielding a central, shallow lagoon.

Green and humid
The steep sides of the island are covered with a lush blanket of tropical vegetation.

Volcanic cone
Layers of lava and ash build up from repeated eruptions.

Surface spurs
Deep channels allow the exchange of water and nutrients between a lagoon and the open ocean.

Young coral reef

1 A coral reef starts to grow in shallow waters around the fringes of a volcano rising above the ocean's surface.

Sloping down
The sides of the volcano descend towards the seabed.

Exotic species
Coral reefs are rich habitats teeming with a vast range of wildlife, including amazing fish of all shades.

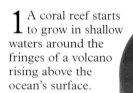

Emperor angelfish   **Royal Gramma**

2 As the surface of the volcano erodes and its base sinks into the ocean, the gap between it and the fringing reef widens into a lagoon. Meanwhile the reef grows upwards. This can also result if the sea level has risen.

Maroon clownfish

Sandy lagoon

Orange sea fan

This gorgonian (horny) coral has a skeleton of long branching arms that allow it to strain food from the water's waving currents.

Scallop shelters in a fold

Scuba playground

Plunging reef walls and caverns are perfect sites for divers to explore the extraordinary colours and shapes of coral formations.

Home for scallops

Although not a true coral, rose coral is a leaf-like colony of many tiny animals growing on the seabed.

Tentacles trap food

Mouth

Stomach cavity

Stony base of polyp skeletons

Green as lettuce
This reef sea slug owes its bizarre colour to the algae that it eats.

Layer upon layer

Colonies of hard coral polyps are linked by a layer of soft tissue. They are hosts to single-celled algae, on which they depend. They also catch plankton from the water.

Seaplane flying overhead

Marine park

Australia's Great Barrier Reef, the largest reef in the world, stretches for 2,028 km (1,260 miles) along the Queensland coast.

4 Now the flattened top of the volcano has vanished beneath the ocean's surface, and coral grows over it. Vegetation has gradually colonized the small atoll islands ringing the lagoon.

Queen angelfish

Reef wall

3 The process goes on as described, with small outcrops of coral appearing inside the lagoon. Where the surface of the reef is uncovered at low tides, fine material is gradually deposited until sandy islands are formed in patches.

Flame angelfish

Falls and rapids

Dramatic waterfalls and cascades, raging rapids, and gaping canyons are river features that have always captivated our imagination and inspired awe. These features form in various ways. Spectacular falls can occur where a river shoots over the edge of a hard-rock ledge or plateau, or over the lip of a glacially carved "hanging valley" onto a plain or valley floor beneath. Meanwhile, glistening cascades or turbulent rapids form where rivers are forced over and around obstructive outcrops or steps of resistant bedrock.

Churning torrents
Water spills over the falls in a misty, thundering barrage. Some falls can be extremely high, the biggest drop in the world being the Angel Falls in Venezuela, South America, which plunges 979 m (3,212 ft) down.

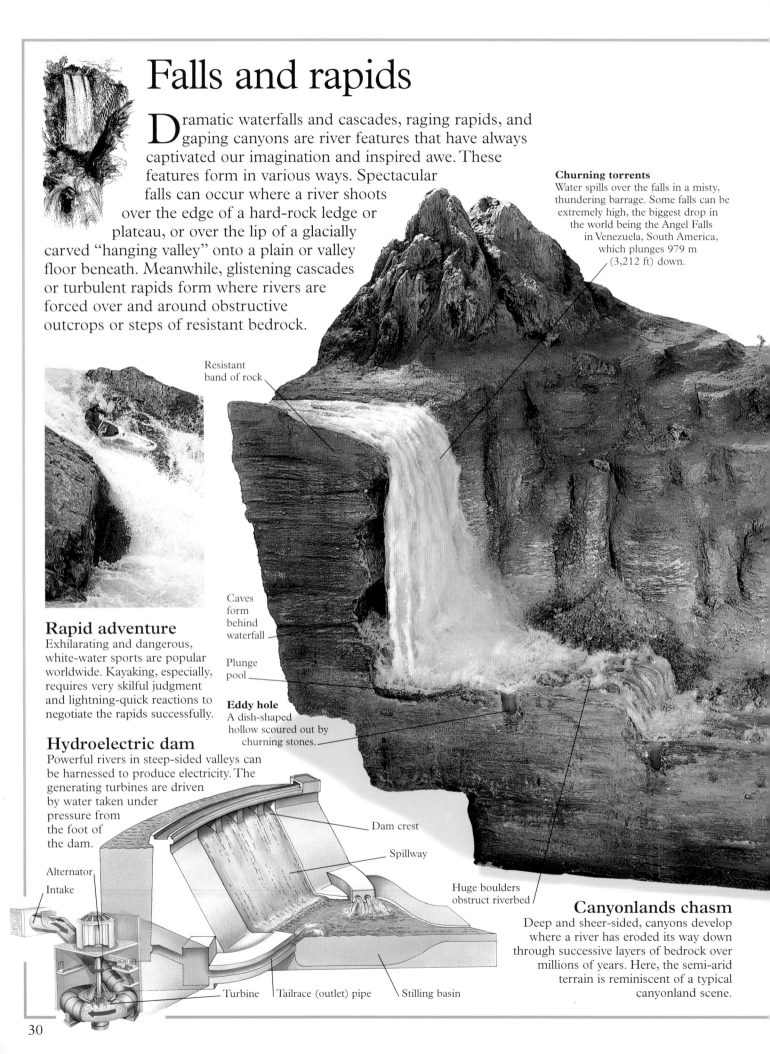

Resistant band of rock

Caves form behind waterfall

Plunge pool

Eddy hole
A dish-shaped hollow scoured out by churning stones.

Rapid adventure
Exhilarating and dangerous, white-water sports are popular worldwide. Kayaking, especially, requires very skilful judgment and lightning-quick reactions to negotiate the rapids successfully.

Hydroelectric dam
Powerful rivers in steep-sided valleys can be harnessed to produce electricity. The generating turbines are driven by water taken under pressure from the foot of the dam.

Alternator

Intake

Dam crest

Spillway

Huge boulders obstruct riverbed

Turbine

Tailrace (outlet) pipe

Stilling basin

Canyonlands chasm
Deep and sheer-sided, canyons develop where a river has eroded its way down through successive layers of bedrock over millions of years. Here, the semi-arid terrain is reminiscent of a typical canyonland scene.

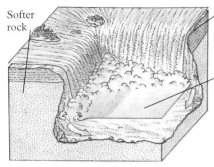

Softer rock

Edge of hard rock band forms lip over which water pours.

Plunge pool
Rocks swirling around in the turbulent water gouge out a bowl-shaped depression at the foot of the falls.

Moving backwards
Falls are constantly retreating upstream in a continuous cycle. Softer rock underlying the resistant band erodes away a cavity with a rocky roof that eventually collapses.

Massive volume
At 108 m (355 ft) the Victoria Falls in Zimbabwe are not the highest in the world, but certainly the largest in terms of the amount of water they carry.

Flowing staircase
The Trappstegsforsen, or "step stream" cascade, flows through a forest in Swedish Lapland. It is a smaller-scale example of how bedrock structure can control a river's course, converting it into a splendid series of watery terraces.

Fallen rock
Canyon walls are scarred by gulleys where debris has fallen, leaving cones of boulders piled up at the river's edge.

Green edges
Small bushes and other plants grow among the rocks in the moist riverbank environment.

Successive red sandstone rock strata is exposed

Only sparse vegetation exists on higher, and drier, surrounding land

Mighty leaps
For salmon returning to their upstream spawning grounds, falls present the ultimate in acrobatic challenges.

Moist cover
Typical vegetation edging waterfalls and riverbanks in temperate zones include ferns and mosses.

Fern

White water
Rapids shoot over debris dams of huge boulders, with calmer water between each dam.

31

Limestone caves

The landforms on and under the Earth's surface are related to the kind of rock from which they are formed. One very distinctive example occurs where water flows through limestone, which is made up of blocks, like bricks in a wall. Water slowly penetrates the joints in between the blocks and, because the rock is sensitive to attack by chemicals in the water, it gradually dissolves. Over time, powerful rivers can excavate vast subterranean cave systems, silent worlds of majestic and mysterious caverns, galleries and deep, menacing shafts.

Exploring a lofty cavern

Birth of a pothole
Water gradually seeps through joints in the rock, dissolving the rock and forming cracks that widen over time into potholes.

Cave dwellers
Bats often live in colonies and sleep during the day in the safety of dark caverns, emerging only at night to feed.

Lesser horseshoe bats

Amazing shapes
As well as pillar-shaped stalagmites and stalactites, many other bizarre and beautiful formations adorn caverns and galleries, including curtains and folds like these in Cox's Cave at Cheddar, Somerset, England.

Steep channel carved by stream

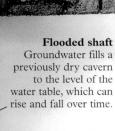

Flooded shaft
Groundwater fills a previously dry cavern to the level of the water table, which can rise and fall over time.

Holes in the ground
Dramatic dolines, or sinkholes, like this one at Totes Gebirge, Austria, which is 20 m (22 yards) deep, are surface depressions caused by water dissolving the rock from above or by cave roofs falling in.

Inside layers
Slicing through a stalactite reveals bands caused by sequences of mineral deposits. The lighter and darker shades of the bands indicate the varying amount of impurities present in the deposits, the lightest being the most pure.

Down under
A typical limestone cave system is shown in this model. The hillside is characteristically bare since limestone offers little moisture and nutrients for lush vegetation. High up, the rock surface has been scraped clean by glacial action, forming a limestone pavement scarred by deep grooves.

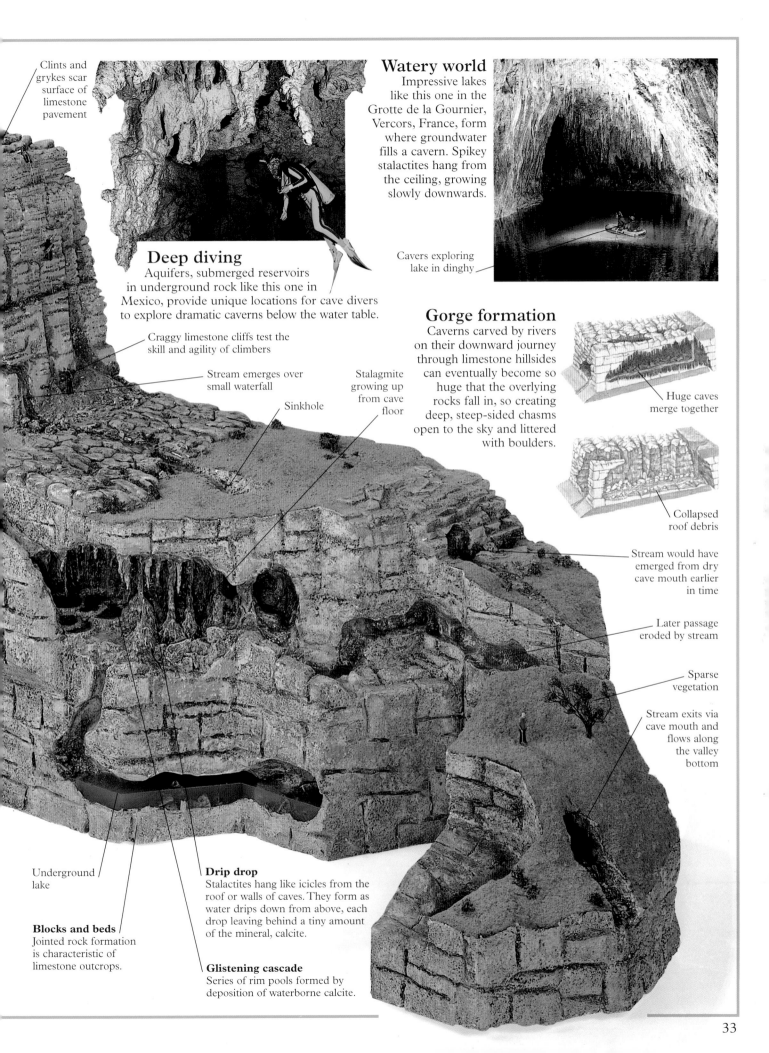

Clints and grykes scar surface of limestone pavement

Watery world

Impressive lakes like this one in the Grotte de la Gournier, Vercors, France, form where groundwater fills a cavern. Spikey stalactites hang from the ceiling, growing slowly downwards.

Cavers exploring lake in dinghy

Deep diving

Aquifers, submerged reservoirs in underground rock like this one in Mexico, provide unique locations for cave divers to explore dramatic caverns below the water table.

Craggy limestone cliffs test the skill and agility of climbers

Stream emerges over small waterfall

Sinkhole

Stalagmite growing up from cave floor

Gorge formation

Caverns carved by rivers on their downward journey through limestone hillsides can eventually become so huge that the overlying rocks fall in, so creating deep, steep-sided chasms open to the sky and littered with boulders.

Huge caves merge together

Collapsed roof debris

Stream would have emerged from dry cave mouth earlier in time

Later passage eroded by stream

Sparse vegetation

Stream exits via cave mouth and flows along the valley bottom

Underground lake

Blocks and beds
Jointed rock formation is characteristic of limestone outcrops.

Drip drop
Stalactites hang like icicles from the roof or walls of caves. They form as water drips down from above, each drop leaving behind a tiny amount of the mineral, calcite.

Glistening cascade
Series of rim pools formed by deposition of waterborne calcite.

Floodplains and deltas

As they travel towards lower land and the sea, rivers transport water and material from the hills and mountains in their upper reaches. The water collects in a river basin, or watershed. Small streams know as tributaries feed the main river. As the mass of water and suspended sediment, together with sand and gravel, moves towards lower ground, the gradient of the river levels out and the entire valley widens. Here a river may start to wander, or meander, in gently sweeping arcs, and may burst its banks after periods of very heavy rainfall. Sometimes, at a river's mouth, so much material is deposited that, over time, a delta is born. In some cases, deltas extend hundreds of kilometres out to sea.

During the 19th century, sailing down the Nile on a dhow like this was much favoured by rich tourists.

War against water
All great rivers are prone to flooding. To protect people and property from this risk, artifical banks, or levees, and a complex series of water control mechanisms, have been built along the Mississippi River in the United States.

Boggy wetlands
Marshes and swamps form where rivers flow over low-lying land. Waterlogged and overgrown, they are a haven for wildfowl in particular.

Stagnant water spread over a wide area

Sharp teeth
Alligators are among the most feared residents of tropical swamps, owing to their silent approach and gaping jaws.

Steamy tropics
This luxuriant cypress swamp near Fort Myers in Florida, United States, is typical of the low-lying coastline bordering the Gulf of Mexico. These are important habitats thriving with an abundance of aquatic plants and wildlife.

Raised banks of distributaries are called levees

Mediterranean Sea

Nile delta

Red Sea

Diverse uses
The papyrus reed, which grows extensively along the Nile valley and in the Nile delta, was used by the ancient Egyptians to make writing parchment and also for building simple boats.

Head of the Nile
The Nile River flows through the Egyptian desert towards its wide, arc-shaped delta. Ever since ancient times, its waters have enabled people to prosper along its banks. If it wasn't for the Nile, the mighty pharoahs would never have existed.

River mouth

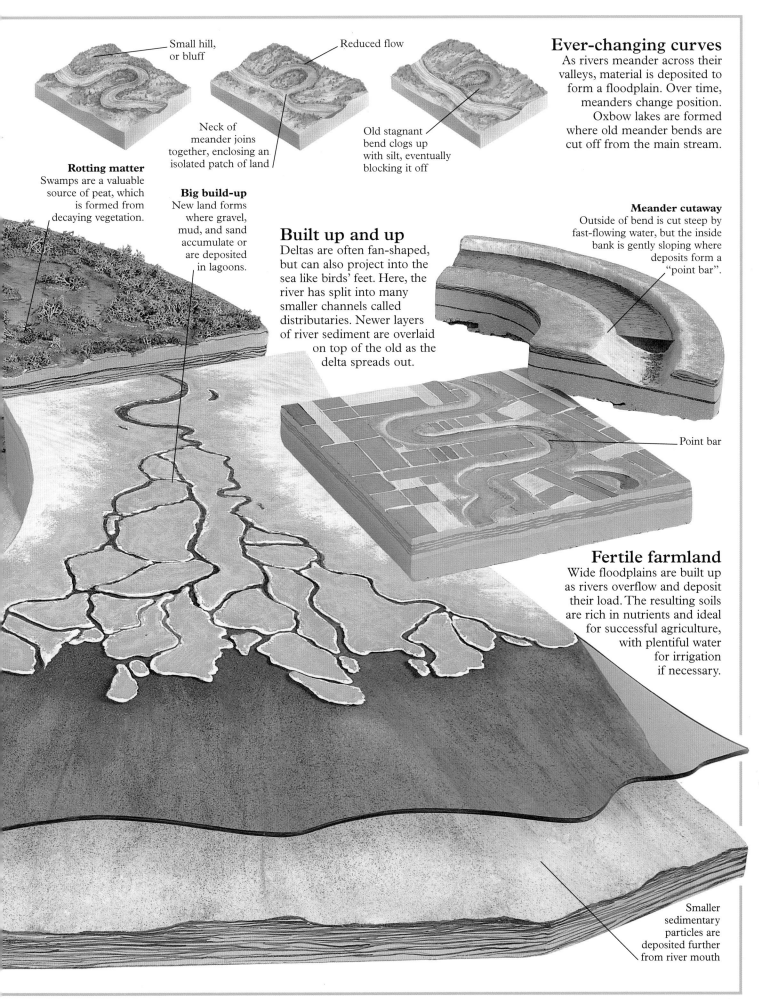

Small hill, or bluff

Reduced flow

Rotting matter
Swamps are a valuable source of peat, which is formed from decaying vegetation.

Neck of meander joins together, enclosing an isolated patch of land

Old stagnant bend clogs up with silt, eventually blocking it off

Big build-up
New land forms where gravel, mud, and sand accumulate or are deposited in lagoons.

Ever-changing curves
As rivers meander across their valleys, material is deposited to form a floodplain. Over time, meanders change position. Oxbow lakes are formed where old meander bends are cut off from the main stream.

Built up and up
Deltas are often fan-shaped, but can also project into the sea like birds' feet. Here, the river has split into many smaller channels called distributaries. Newer layers of river sediment are overlaid on top of the old as the delta spreads out.

Meander cutaway
Outside of bend is cut steep by fast-flowing water, but the inside bank is gently sloping where deposits form a "point bar".

Point bar

Fertile farmland
Wide floodplains are built up as rivers overflow and deposit their load. The resulting soils are rich in nutrients and ideal for successful agriculture, with plentiful water for irrigation if necessary.

Smaller sedimentary particles are deposited further from river mouth

Desert lands

Desert rose
Intriguing petal-shaped crystals like this form when gypsum dust dissolves in rainwater or water trapped in sand dunes.

Arid and desolate, deserts are full of surprises. For example, while many occur in the hot, tropical areas of the world, some also exist in colder, mountainous regions. Formed where more rainfall evaporates than falls, most deserts feature rocky uplands and barren plains, rather than great 'seas' of sand. When the rains do come to desert lands, flash floods can occur. These bring seeds that have lain dormant in the ground for many years suddenly into bloom, transforming the dry landscape into a blanket of colour.

Ships of the desert

Pyramid stone
Even small stones and pebbles are shaped and their surfaces varnished by sand blasting. This three-sided example is called a dreikanter.

Palm trees encircle oasis

Desert nomads camp

Aquifer rock

Water seeps up fault in rock

Welcome water
Many deserts conceal aquifers, reserves of rainwater trapped in underground rocks. Where this water reaches the surface, an oasis or desert pond appears, and plants can grow.

Hamada
Hostile desert plain strewn with small rocks or gravel.

Inselberg
Solitary rocky hill in the desert plain.

Rock arch
An impressive formation sculpted by the wind from a protruding fin of rock.

Tapering walls
The skirt, or pediment, of the plateau has deep gulleys gouged out by past rains.

Spines and ripples
Prevailing winds shape the sand seas, or ergs, of Saharan Africa into massive dune fields. Pictured here are long, narrow "seif" dunes; other forms are crescent- and star-shaped.

Shifting sands
Sand dunes are constantly on the move, blown in the same direction as the wind (blue arrow). This cross-section shows how old dune structures are overlaid and compacted by younger ones.

Gulleys and fans
Rocky outcrops like this one in Mungo National Park, Australia, are often scarred by deep gashes carved by rainwater. At their bases lie fan-shaped deposits of mud and silt.

Desert tombstones
This field of sand-blasted rock pinnacles is in the Namburg National Park in Australia. The wind has worn down the outer layers of rock, leaving only columns and plinths of harder material. The effect is one of a silent, scorching graveyard.

Barrel cactus

Spikes deter predators

Water bearers
Desert cacti conserve water by storing it in their fleshy tissue. Shallow roots spread out to absorb whatever rain or dew there is.

Water-storing tissue

Dry wadi
River channel carved during wetter climatic conditions in the past.

Rock strata clearly visible in cliff face

Pinnacles of snow
High altitude, or mountain, deserts like the Atacama desert in Chile, are dry wildernesses where all moisture is locked into ice. Here, snow has frozen into spikey pillars awaiting the summer sun.

Desert plateau
Upland outcrops are gradually shrinking. The encircling cliffs are being worn down by a combination of wind, sand, extreme temperature variations, rainwater, and chemical processes.

Fast mover
Desert creatures have adapted to the environment in amazing ways. This lizard's long claws have a fringe of scales to stop it sinking into the hot sand.

Fallen boulders litter dry river bed

Mesa

Butte

Towers and tables
The striking mesas and buttes of the dry, rock-strewn plain of Monument Valley, Arizona, United States, are all that remain of a vast plateau. The encircling rock has been eroded away.

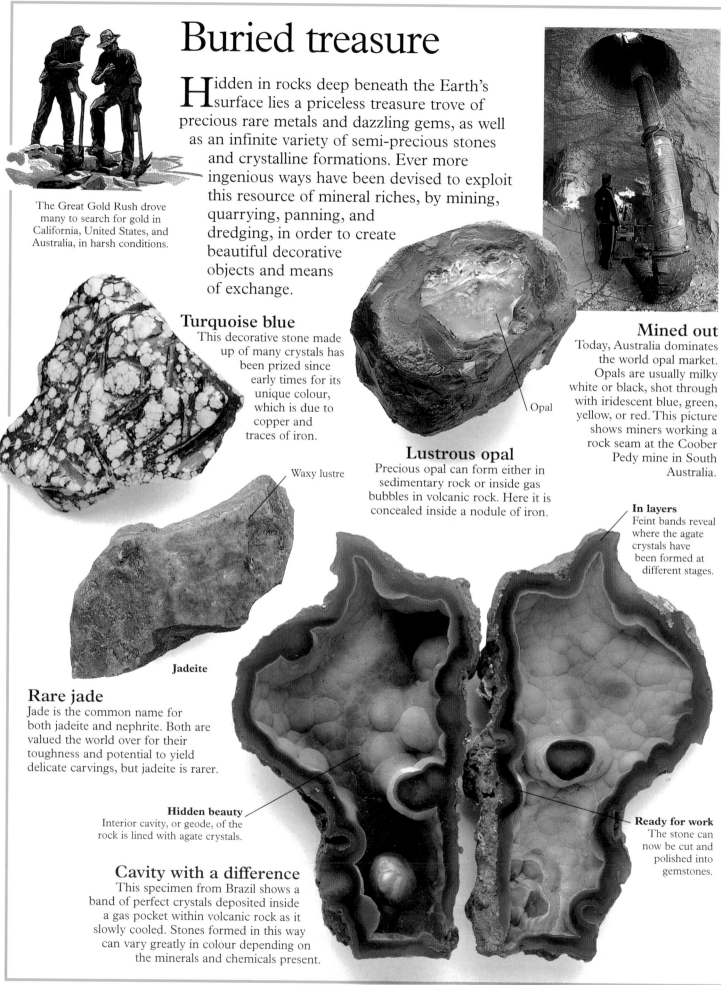

Buried treasure

Hidden in rocks deep beneath the Earth's surface lies a priceless treasure trove of precious rare metals and dazzling gems, as well as an infinite variety of semi-precious stones and crystalline formations. Ever more ingenious ways have been devised to exploit this resource of mineral riches, by mining, quarrying, panning, and dredging, in order to create beautiful decorative objects and means of exchange.

The Great Gold Rush drove many to search for gold in California, United States, and Australia, in harsh conditions.

Turquoise blue
This decorative stone made up of many crystals has been prized since early times for its unique colour, which is due to copper and traces of iron.

Lustrous opal
Precious opal can form either in sedimentary rock or inside gas bubbles in volcanic rock. Here it is concealed inside a nodule of iron.

Opal

Mined out
Today, Australia dominates the world opal market. Opals are usually milky white or black, shot through with iridescent blue, green, yellow, or red. This picture shows miners working a rock seam at the Coober Pedy mine in South Australia.

Waxy lustre

In layers
Feint bands reveal where the agate crystals have been formed at different stages.

Jadeite

Rare jade
Jade is the common name for both jadeite and nephrite. Both are valued the world over for their toughness and potential to yield delicate carvings, but jadeite is rarer.

Hidden beauty
Interior cavity, or geode, of the rock is lined with agate crystals.

Ready for work
The stone can now be cut and polished into gemstones.

Cavity with a difference
This specimen from Brazil shows a band of perfect crystals deposited inside a gas pocket within volcanic rock as it slowly cooled. Stones formed in this way can vary greatly in colour depending on the minerals and chemicals present.

"The Big Hole"

This deep chasm is an old diamond mine in Kimberley, South Africa. South Africa is a major supplier of diamonds, and is home to De Beers, the firm that regulates the world diamond market.

Kashmir blue

Like ruby, sapphire is a variety of the mineral, corundum. Sapphire describes a blue stone like the one above, but other colours include yellow, pink, and gold.

Ruskin's ruby

Donated to the Natural History Museum in London by the philosopher John Ruskin in 1887, this Burmese ruby crystal possesses a richness of colour found only in the highest quality gems.

Hard nut
Diamond embedded in a lump of volcanic rock.

Diamond

The strength and durability of diamonds, along with their great lustre and "fire", make them the most prized jewels in the world.

Aquamarine

This blue-green variety of beryl takes its name from the colour of the sea. Beryl has been mined since ancient times, and also comes in yellow (heliodor) and pink (morganite) varieties.

Emerald crystal

Granite

Swirling action

Gold can be found in the beds of rivers and streams. This 1908 painting shows a prospector panning for heavy grains and nuggets.

Rich veins

Gold is valued both for jewellery and in some industrial processes. It is often found in incrustations within veins of quartz.

Green beryl

Known as emerald, this is the most famous of beryl varieties. Spanish invaders first came across emeralds in the early 1500s, amongst the treasures of the Incas of Peru and the Aztecs of Mexico.

Laborious process
A worker carts off the gold ore to be crushed; the residue will then be smelted.

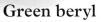

Light-sensitive metal

Silver is currently used for many purposes, including coatings on photographic paper and films. One of the first rare metals to be discovered, it is prone to tarnishing, which may explain why it has never been as valuable as gold.

Platinum

This precious and malleable metal is now more valuable than gold.

Danger zone

Early gold mining was labour-intensive and the mines were hazardous places to work in, with poor ventilation and the constant threat of tunnel collapse.

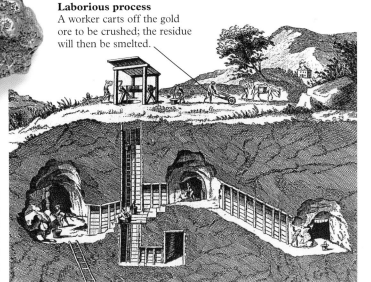

Caring for the Earth

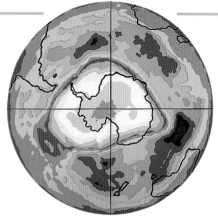

The Earth is not large, and its supply of natural resources not limitless. Despite this we are exploiting the planet more than ever before. Already at almost 6 billion, global population is rising by 120 million each year; as a result, energy consumption is increasing, as is the sum of industrial and agricultural waste. If the environment is to survive, we must nurture the Earth better. Use of energy and raw materials must be carefully planned. Waste disposal, especially of toxic substances, must be made safe, so the land and oceans are not polluted. It is also our duty to protect the Earth's great abundance of natural habitats and wildlife, for future generations to enjoy.

Window over Antarctica
The Earth's ozone layer protects us from harmful solar radiation. It is not certain what causes the "hole" in this layer (the pink area in the satellite image above) that occurs over Antarctica in spring. However, pollution in the atmosphere has been suggested.

Arctic garbage dump
Refuse from industrialized zones is washed up on remote Arctic coasts, demonstrating the global nature of sea pollution. Plastic, especially, is not easily broken down by natural processes, and will pollute the environment for many years.

Dried-out former seabed

Bare plains
In typical areas of desertification, most of the sparse tree cover has been felled for fuel, which exposes the topsoil.

Raw sewage
Discharge into rivers and seas is still a common way of disposing of sewage. Tighter laws controlling water quality, however, are gradually changing this practice.

An unquenchable thirst
This fishing boat in Uzbekistan, central Asia, has been stranded as the Aral Sea has receded. Over the last 30 years, so much river water that used to enter the lake has been diverted for irrigation that it has shrunk to half its former size.

Encroaching deserts
Where grasslands are under pressure from soil erosion, over-grazing, and climatic fluctuations, the need for soil conservation is acute. The Sahel region of Africa, bordering the southern edges of the Sahara desert, is particularly under threat; in some areas, the desert has advanced 350 km (220 miles) in just 20 years.

One big cover-up

Modern landfill methods of garbage disposal are carefully designed to prevent groundwater contamination and the build-up of inflammable gases. Any toxic substances, together with rainwater (this compound is called "leachate") are pumped out of the pit.

Natural landscape cover

Leachate pool

Pipes around site monitor groundwater quality

Network of pipes allows dangerous gases to escape

Each day's refuse sealed with a layer of earth

Driven by the wind
Wind turbines are the successors of the traditional windmill, their blades rotating like huge propellors.

Pumping station
Shape of pit allows leachate to percolate along looser gravel layer towards a central sump. From here it is pumped out and transported elsewhere for safe and effective disposal.

Pit lining

Layers of compacted earth

Gravel layer

Thick waterproof plastic sheeting

Jungle butterflies from South America

Gardens of Eden
Rainforests support a huge diversity of plants and wildlife. These ecosystems must be preserved and new forest economies created.

The search for renewable energy
In view of the Earth's dwindling fossil fuel reserves, new sources of energy must be found. Power can be generated by the wind (left), the tides, the Sun (solar power), and volcanic underground heat, as in Iceland (right).

River restoration
Over the last ten years, major efforts have been made to rejuvenate river and stream environments in industrial zones.

Slag heaps

New, winding river course created

Gravel laid to encourage fish and water beetles to breed and new food chains to be created

River area widened

Under threat
The Earth's most precious habitats are its tropical forests. As trees are felled, the topsoil degrades rapidly. New logging methods, including replanting and other effective forest management techniques, are gradually being introduced around the world.

Forest floor has plentiful prey

Trees and shrubs planted along banks

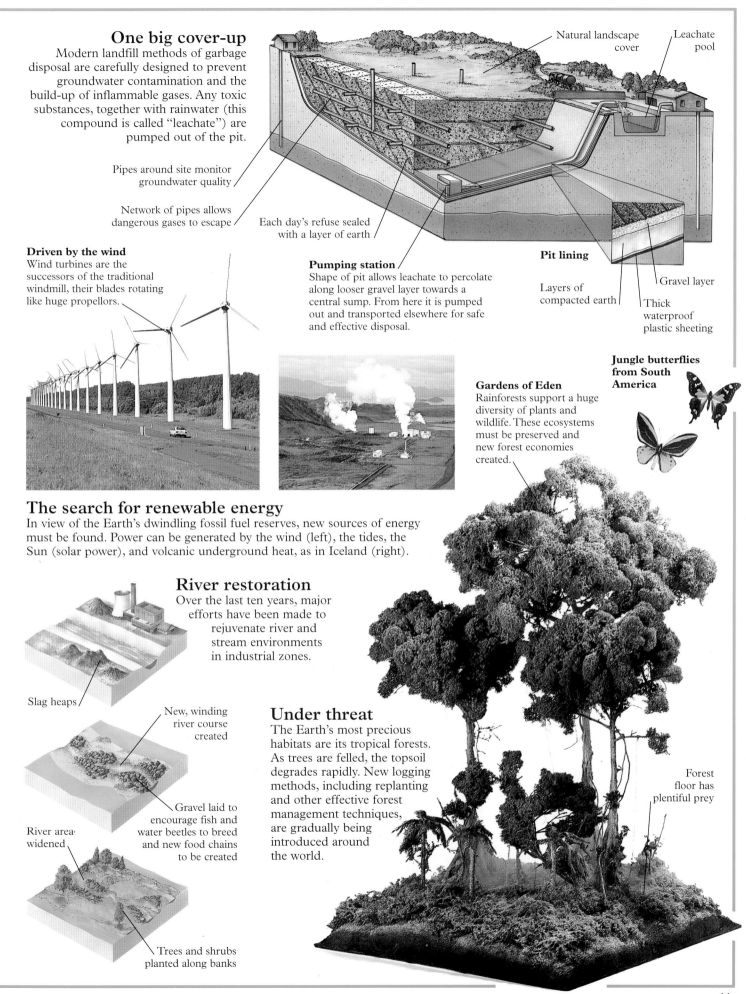

Glossary

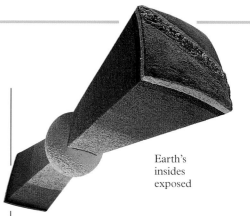

Earth's insides exposed

A

Abyssal plain The deep, flatter part of the ocean floors, often covered with scattered lumps, or nodules, of the metallic element manganese.

Algae Simple-structured plants that may be minute or a huge seaweed. Algae contain chlorophyll and manufacture their own food using sunlight.

Alternator An electrical device that creates an alternating current, that is one which rapidly changes direction.

Aquifer A layer of rock trapping water underground.

Arctic The ice-covered area surrounding the North Pole.

B

Bacteria A large group of usually single-celled micro-organisms.

Bedrock Solid rock layers beneath the soil and surface cove of the Earth.

C

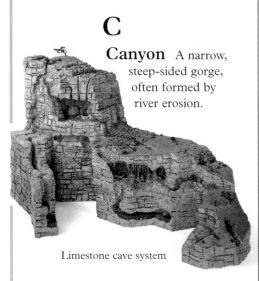

Canyon A narrow, steep-sided gorge, often formed by river erosion.

Limestone cave system

Clints and grykes Eroded ridges and grooves in limestone surfaces.

Cavitation A "shock-hammer" effect in which bubbles form and collapse in very fast-flowing water, causing rapid variations in pressure and resulting in considerable erosion.

Continental drift Horizontal movements of the Earth's crust responsible for the present arrangement of the continents. Theory first published in 1915 by the German meteorologist Alfred Wegener (1880–1930).

Crevasse A deep crack or split in the surface of a glacier or ice sheet.

Crustaceans A group of animals with an external shell split into segments.

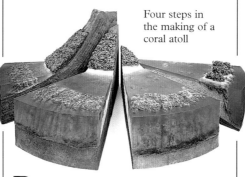

Four steps in the making of a coral atoll

D

Distributary Small channel on a river delta taking water from a main river to lakes or the sea.

Doldrums A belt of low atmospheric pressure surrounding the equator. Mariners of old dreaded the doldrums as their vessels could be becalmed for lengthy periods.

F

Fissure A crack in the side of a volcano through which lava escapes. The term also refers to a crack in any surface.

Fossil fuels These include natural gas, crude oil, and coal, all of which occur naturally and are formed from the decomposition of prehistoric organisms.

G

Gastropod A type of mollusc, or shell-dwelling animal, often with a coiled shell – a snail for example.

Great Barrier Reef This lies off Australia's northeast coast, and is the longest coral reef in the world. It has taken about 800 million years to build, and is home to over 400 types of coral and 1,500 species of fish.

Great Gold Rush This most famous gold rush occurred after gold was first discovered in the US state of California in 1848 by John Marshall. People flocked from the eastern United States and Europe in search of their fortunes. A similar rush took place in the wake of gold being discovered in Australia in 1851. Further gold rushes happened in later years and also in Canada, New Zealand, and South Africa.

Guyot A mountain on the ocean bed, with a characteristic flat top that would once have been an island.

H

Hanging valley A tributary valley that enters its main river valley high up on one side, often creating a waterfall.

L

Limestone A calcium-rich rock often formed as fresh or salt-water has evaporated or as shelly creatures have died and accumulated on sea and lake beds.

River falls and rapids

M

Mineral An inorganic substance with a simple chemical form. Minerals are found in combination in rocks.

Molluscs A group of invertebrate animals with shells.

Moulin A vertical pipe or shaft carrying water and rocks from the surface to the bed of a glacier.

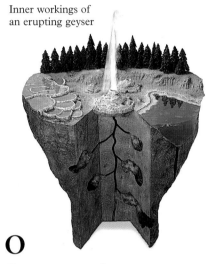

Inner workings of an erupting geyser

O

Ocean trench The deep troughs or valleys on the floor of the oceans. The deepest trenches occur at subduction zones, where oceanic and continental crust converges.

Ores Metal-bearing rocks that can be mined and then processed to extract the pure metal.

P

Panning Technique for separating grains of valuble mineral ores from riverbed sand and gravel by washing the material in a pan using a swirling action.

Plankton Very small (often microscopic) organisms that float in marine and freshwater environments. They may be animal, plant, or bacterial in origin.

Pumice A very light volcanic rock that water can easily penetrate, which is formed as steams and gases escaped from cooling lava.

Q

Quartz A common, usually glassy mineral formed from silicon and oxygen. Pulverized quartz makes up the bulk of sand.

R

Richter scale System for measuring the intensity, or magnitude, of an earthquake, based upon readings taken from a seismograph, which records ground motion. Named after the US seismologist Charles Richter (1900–1985), who developed it in 1935.

S

Sahara The world's largest desert, stretching over 5,500 km (3,410 miles) east to west across North Africa and almost 2,000 km (1,240 miles) north to south). It is almost totally barren apart from scattered oases and the banks of the River Nile.

Sand dune A massive accumulation of sand, blown and shaped by the wind into a hill or ridge.

Sandstone A rock formed from grains of sand cemented together by silica or calcium carbonate.

Satellite Man-made devices that continuously orbit the Earth in space. They have many uses, including communications, weather forecasts, marine and aircraft navigation, and keeping track of military exercises on the ground.

Slice through a blasting volcano

Solar radiation Energy received from the Sun which drives the Earth's weather and climatic circulation. The energy is generated by nuclear reactions taking place inside the Sun itself. Amazingly, the entire population of the Earth uses as much energy in one year as the Sun delivers to the Earth in under an hour.

T

Temperate zone A mid-latitude zone of the Earth, away from continental areas, which is marked by warm and cool seasons.

Tributary A river or stream that feeds its water into a larger river or river system.

Tropics The region of the Earth centred on the equator, lying between 23.5° N and S, and characterized by hot weather throughout the year.

W

Wadi A dry river channel in a desert area which contains water only after heavy rainfall.

Watershed The boundary between the headwaters of two merging river systems. In the US, the term is used to describe a river basin.

Black smokers in the ocean depths

Index

Acknowledgements

The publisher would like to thank:
BBC Visual Effects, for their enthusiasm in making the models: Andrew David, Malcolm James, Mike Tucker, Colin Mapson, Alan Marshall, Alison Jeffrey, Nick Kool

Author's consultant: Dr John French, Geography Department, University College London

Design assistance: Rachael Dyson, Iain Morris, Salesh Patel, Susan St Louis, Jason Gonzalez, Emma Bowden

Editorial assistance: Julie Ferris

Photoshop retouching:
Bob Warner and Oblong Box

Visualization: Martyn Foote

Illustrations: 8bl Peter Bull Art Studio; 9br Colin Salmon; 11cr, br, 14l, 18bl, 20br, 25tr, 30bl (turbine by Rick Blakeley), 35t, 36c Mike Saunders; 8tr Richard Ward; 9tr, 12tr, 19bl, 23tr, 29cl, 41tr, bl John Woodcock; 11cl David Ashby; 10c, 15br, 36bl Richard Bonson;16l, 31tl Colin Rose; 12–13 (except 12tr) Will Giles & Sandra Pond; 22tr Luciano Corbella; 33cr Nick Hall

Additional models: 10 Dave Donkin; 14–15, 36–37, 41br Donks Models; 24–25, 34–35 Peter Griffiths

Picture Credits
Key: l=left, r=right, t=top, c=centre, a=above, b=below

Nick Clifford: 20cr; 21tl **Mary Evans Picture Library:** 16tl; 38tl; 39br; 39cl **Geoscience:** 17tr; 18crb; 32bl; 33tr; 34cla **Robert Harding Picture Library:** / Michael Botham 26cl; 20tr; 20cl; 32cl; 39tl **The Image Bank:** 10br; /Jeff Hunter 29tl; /Stefano Scato 29cr **Frank Lane Picture Agency:** /D Fleetham/ Silvestris 28tr; /Mark Newman 30cl; /W Wisniewsk 23tr; 31tc; 34cl; 40cr **Mansell Collection:** 8tl **Oxford Scientific Films:** /David Curl 26cr; /Ben Osborne 22cl, 23tl; /Richard Packwood 18cla **Photo © Jerry Young:** 34cla **Planet Earth:** /John R Bracegirdle 27br; /John Fawcett 18tr;

21tr; /Robert Hessler 24cl; 25c; /Jan Jove Johansson 31tr; 36clb; 37br; /Doug Perrine 33tl; Jonathon Scott 22bl; /William Smithey 25cr; 27br; /Verena Tunnicliffe 25cl **Science Photo Library:** 10cl; 10-11; /Martin Bond 41cl; /Douglas Faulkner 28cl; 34bc; /Simon Fraser 37cra; 40c; 40cl; 41c; /Gordon Garradd 36br; /John Mead 37tl; /Peter Meizel 15tr, 15cr; 38tr; /Nasa 8clb; /David Parker 14tr; /Roger Ressmeyer/Starlight 16tr; /US Geological Survey 15tl; /John Wells 40tl **Frank Spooner Pictures:** 17br

Index: Marion Dent